That's a Good Question

Philippa Werry

illustrated by
Jacob Laumanuvae

Mom, Kelly, and I were driving to the pool. Kelly asked, "Has the pool always been called The Nonstop Fun Swimming Pool?"

"That's a good question," said Mom. "When I was young, there was a guy in our town called Johnny Fun. He told his brother that he could swim the length of the pool. His brother didn't believe him."

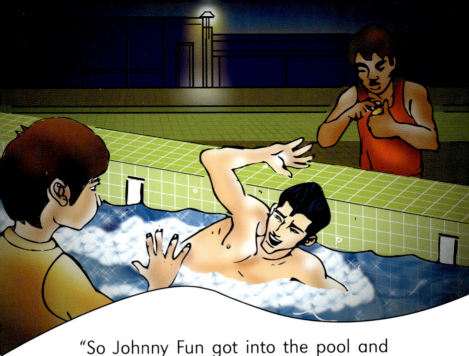

"So Johnny Fun got into the pool and swam the length one time.
His brother was amazed.
Johnny swam two lengths,
then three lengths.
His brother was even more amazed,
but Johnny Fun didn't stop.
He just kept swimming –
ten, twenty, thirty lengths.
Closing time came, but Johnny Fun kept on swimming," said Mom.

"The lifeguard dove into the pool to
pull him out,
but every time he tried to grab him,
Johnny Fun somehow slipped away
and kept on swimming.
They called his parents,
but Johnny Fun kept on swimming.
He swam all night,
and the next morning,
he was still swimming," said Mom.

"What happened next?" I asked.

"That's a good question," said Mom.

"The next evening,
he was still swimming.
By then, the newspapers and
the TV networks
had heard about him.
They sent reporters and camera crews.
Johnny was on the national news.
People came from all over
to watch him.
A billboard went up outside the pool,
showing how many lengths he'd swum."

"Didn't he run out of energy?" asked Kelly.

"That's a good question," said Mom. "Every so often, he would swim backstroke. A pool attendant squirted orange juice into his mouth. Another pool attendant tossed candy into his mouth."

"Didn't Johnny get bored?" I asked.

"That's a good question," said Mom.

"Johnny Fun seemed quite happy.
His brother ran up and down the side
of the pool shouting 'I believe you!',
but Johnny just smiled and waved."

"What happened in the end?"
asked Kelly.

"Now, that's a good question,"
said Mom.
"Johnny Fun swam slower and slower.
After a week,
it took him most of the day
just to swim one length.
Finally, he stopped.
He became known as Johnny Nonstop
Fun. The pool was named after him."

Mom drove into the pool's parking lot. "Mom," I asked as we got out of the car, "is that a true story?"

"Now, that's a good question," said Mom.